Devotions
for the
Alcoholic
Christian

CARL NELSON

C.S.S. Publishing Co., Inc.
Lima, Ohio

DEVOTIONS FOR THE ALCOHOLIC CHRISTIAN

Library of Congress Cataloging-in-Publication Data

Nelson, Carl, 1934-
   Devotions for the alcoholic Christian.

   1. Alcoholics — Prayer-books and devotions — English. I. Title.
BV4596.A48N45   1988   242'.66   87-30155
ISBN 1-55673-033-0 (pbk.)

Second Printing November 1990

8817 / ISBN 1-55673-033-0

The author and publisher wish to underscore the fact that the names Bill and Betty are fictitious. The incidents recorded represent composites of many different real cases known to the author.

Getting Acquainted

How does a Christian even get started drinking excessively? What does a Christian do with the overwhelming guilt over deeds done while drunk? What happened to God when I prayed so earnestly for him to help me not to take the next drink? How can I resume my role as a member of a congregation that is so aware of what I was like while drinking? These and many other questions plague the Christian alcoholic. Answers are not always easy to come by, especially as he searches for Christ-centered literature. Most of the material deals with some spiritual aspects of alcoholism, but not necessarily from a Christian point of view. And some Christian material seems to center on the moralistic and legalistic approaches to the problem.

This little devotional booklet is this author's attempt to offer the suffering Christian alcoholic some insight into his problem, a way of finding spiritual reconciliation and peace with God, a renewed sense of worth within the household of faith, and an opportunity to reestablish himself as a functional member of the body of Christ.

References will be made to fictional persons named "Bill" and Betty," who are composites of many real life people whom the author has had the pleasure of knowing over these past years. Though "Bill" and "Betty" are fictional, the stories told of their experience are true, simply changed enough to prevent accidental identification of the real persons behind the stories.

The author is also grateful to many friends in the programs of Alcoholics Anonymous and Al-Anon whose power of example shows what life can be like for the alcoholic and his family, both before and after sobriety. The Twelve Step program used by these groups forms the basic outline for these devotions. It is hoped that in this way the recovering alcoholic will be better able to wed his Christian faith and his program of recovery.

With the realization that nothing on this earth is perfect, any suggestions for improvements for this booklet will be most welcome and will be considered for any later revision. May God bless you in your meditations and study of his precious Word.

First Day

(Newcomers to alcoholic recovery are told to just do what is recommended and trust the mind to follow later. One of the suggestions is to begin and end each day with prayer. In the morning, thank God for the protection of the night and ask his guidance for the day. In the evening, thank God for his gifts and guidance for the day and ask for his protection during the night. Each of our morning and evening devotions will begin with prayer. Please find a place where you won't be disturbed and you will receive the greatest benefit.)

Morning

Prayer

Dear heavenly Father, I thank you for watching over me this past night, and for giving me restful and renewing sleep. I thank you for the gift of another day in which I may live in gratitude for your many blessings to me and my loved ones. May your Holy Spirit guide and direct my thoughts, my words, and my actions throughout the hours of this day. Help me to follow in the footsteps of my loving Savior as I serve you this day. Amen

Meditation

Step One of the Alcoholics Anonymous suggested program of recovery tells us that we were powerless over alcohol and that our lives had become unmanageable. Christians are especially conscious of this truth because we have been made aware of God's will for us throughout our Christian lives. At the same time, we also found ourselves trying to rationalize our way between obedience to God and the desire to have just one more drink. We promised God, our loved ones, and ourselves that each time it was going to be different. We kept telling ourselves we could control the drinking. We knew when to stop — and afterwards, knew nothing but remorse and regret!

We compared ourselves to other people and couldn't understand why they could enjoy social drinking without getting into problems. For some of us even the first drink caused us trouble; for others of us it took some time before we realized we were out of control. Why are we so different? Is God punishing us? Is God ignoring us?

Have we ever really considered that we can't achieve perfection? Yes, we've said, "Nobody can be perfect." But as soon as we said that, we reserved for ourselves the right to be the exception. Alcohol proved to us that we can't. A simple chemical could reduce us to all sorts of shameful behavior and lack of responsibility. We finally had to admit that we were powerless. Think of Saint Paul who said that the good he wanted to do he did not, and the evil he didn't want to do he did. Like Saint Paul we are imperfect. We make mistakes. With regard to alcohol, we found out we had another imperfection. We found we were allergic to the chemical alcohol. Just as a diabetic cannot take sugar, we cannot take alcohol. Our sinful pride did not want to admit this at first. We kept trying to prove to ourselves that we were like "normal" people. We kept trying to prove that we could drink "normally." Our own opinion of ourselves stood in the way of reason, and somewhere we crossed the invisible line into addiction. At that point our choices were taken from us. We were powerless, and are powerless, over alcohol!

Under the influence of alcohol we did all sorts of things we ordinarily would not. Some of us had "blackouts," the strange shutting down of the brain's memory banks so that we didn't remember what we did when we drank too much. For some of us, days — even weeks — were lost forever. In many cases, other members of our family took over our responsibilities. But we really didn't mind that, because that allowed us to concentrate more and more on our drinking.

Thank God he permitted us to arrive at a point where we cried out for help in such a way that we were ready to surrender ourselves to someone else. We were indeed powerless and our lives were indeed unmanageable. "Let him that thinks he stands take heed, lest he fall." How prophetic those words of our Savior were for us.

Life Example

Meet "Bill." Bill, I hope, will soon become a familiar figure with whom you may identify. You see, in his drinking days, Bill would find himself in some rather curious situations. Bill also had trouble with his finances. For a long time Bill prided himself on the fact that no matter how much he drank, he never missed a day's work and always brought home the pay. Finally, however, that changed. He always had money for drinks, but sometimes none for food, rent, and other necessities for the family. It seems they didn't really understand him when he tried to explain why.

Other things happened to Bill which he couldn't figure out. Like that time in the morning when he went to get his car out of the garage, and found the door on the driver's side missing. Alcohol has a way of making life interesting.

I remember when Bill was once on a trip and felt the need for just one drink to bolster his spirits in order to apply for a new job. He stopped off at the airport lounge. Four days later, he awoke in a hotel some two thousand miles away — and next to him was his new wife whom he didn't remember ever meeting or marrying! How he got there and what happened during those four days will forever be a mystery to Bill.

Scripture Study

Psalm 31:9-10, Luke 22:39-44, Romans 7:18-24

Personal Meditations:

Evening Devotion

Prayer

Dear Savior, you who have given of yourself even into death for me, I come to you this night grateful for the forgiveness of my sins, grateful for giving me new life, grateful for the gift of your Spirit. Little by little, I am learning to cast all my cares on you. I am learning to let go of my pride and selfishness and be filled with your love. May the angels watch over me this night. May I sleep in peace as you renew my strength for another day. In your name I pray. Amen

Meditation

Little by little we learn that we are not indispensable. Little by little, we learn that the world continues with or without us. Human pride makes us think more highly of ourselves than we ought to think. When we finally realize that apart from God we are nothing, then we are ready to hear God's good news. God tells us in his Word that he has created us anew in Christ Jesus. Through Jesus' death and resurrection, we have been given the opportunity to live a whole new life. The big message of redemption is forgiveness of sin. We have heard those words so much, but hear them again we must. All the remorse, all the guilt, all the fear which had left us so Frustrated, Ego-centered, Angry, and Resentful, are covered by the blood of Jesus.

When we began a program of recovery we learned that alcoholism is a disease. Addictive alcoholics are different from other people. A physical factor has been discovered in them that reacts with alcohol in such a way that the entire neuro-physiological system is altered. Susceptibility is absolute. For such people, alcohol is like a poison that can destroy the will and the decision-making processes of the body and mind. This can be instantaneous for some; for others it may take years.

Even though we may not have been aware of such extreme dangers of drinking too much, we Christians were told that too much drinking would cause problems. Therefore we know that we must bear responsibility for those first drinks. We know also that we must bear the responsibility for our actions "under the influence," even if we are unaware what those actions were. We Christians are able to do that because we also know the source of forgiveness, the atonement of our sins through the blood of Jesus. We can confess the sins of our drinking as no one else can.

Life Example

Bill was a "closet drinker," that is, he tried to hide his drinking from his friends and family. This worked for a while. No one thought that Bill had any problems with alcohol. But, as the drinking progressed, the harder it became to keep his drinking to himself. The signs of the progression became more and more obvious. It was harder to hide his habit. Bill decided to drop out of more and more activities. People began to wonder what happened to Bill. This was especially so in Bill's church. He had served his congregation in many ways. Now he didn't even show up for Sunday worship. When someone from the church called on Bill, he was always cordial, agreed that he had to get back into the swing of things, but never quite fulfilled his promises to the visitors.

When Bill finally faced his problem and was in a program of recovery, he was very much concerned about what his former friends at church thought of him. He felt he couldn't face anyone at church.

But he had a good friend who encouraged him to return and give it a try. Bill sought out one of his former associates on one of the boards and told him his story. That associate looked at Bill and said, "So, what else is new?" Bill found out that they had known he had a problem with alcohol even before he did. He found out that the church had been ready to accept him long before he was ready to accept himself or the church. It was not long before Bill was resuming a fruitful life in his congregation.

Scripture Study

Ephesians 2:1-10, 1 John 1:7-10

Personal Meditations:

Second Day

Morning Devotion

Prayer

Most gracious Father in heaven. Again, I thank you for keeping me this past night from all harm and danger, and for the gift of another day. Let your Word be my guide this day. Send your Spirit to cast aside my doubts and strengthen my faith in you. Give me boldness of heart to turn to you for my every need and to renew my spirit. Keep me close to my Savior throughout this day. Amen

Meditation

Step two asks us to come to believe that a Power greater than ourselves can restore us to sanity. First of all, most of us have trouble with that word "sanity," because we never thought of ourselves as insane. All we have to do, however, is think back to the horrors of the past and ask ourselves if we always chose the course of wisdom. How many times did we choose a foolish course of action simply because our desire for a drink overrode any other thoughts? Perhaps, if we substituted "not thinking straight" for "insane" the concept would be more acceptable.

Now what about the Power greater than ourselves? As Christians we have always claimed a belief in God. How can we *now* ask to believe? What we're talking about here is total dependence on God. Of course, while we were drinking, we often prayed to God to have him stop us from taking that next drink. In the later stages of our decline, we even begged it of him. Genuine honesty demands of us, nevertheless, to admit that even while we were asking these things of God, we were already planning our next drink. We still *believed* *we* were in control.

There is a little formula used to describe human actions. It is $I/E = A$, where "I" is intellect, "E" is emotion, and "A" is action. Usually, our intellect is in control of our emotions as we act out our daily lives. Alcohol robs us of that control. Our emotions ride herd over our intellect, and we find ourselves doing things we would never have done if we were reasonable. Alcohol flipped the formula to read $E/I = A$. That is why no one could meaningfully communicate with us while we were under the influence. We were not reasonable! We were not thinking straight. We were "insane."

Alcohol also warped our faith. It told us to believe in ourselves instead of God. It gave us a false sense of security. It convinced us we could do anything we wanted to do, and we could do it by ourselves. It told us we didn't need anyone — not friends, not family, not God! It convinced us that all we really needed was just one more drink.

Thank God that, though we deserted him, he did not desert us. It was indeed God who led us to our recovery, and now we are asked to acknowledge that fact. We can now come to believe that God can restore us to sanity. We can now come to believe that with God all things are possible. There is no limit to what God can accomplish in us and through us. He has demonstrated his power in the resurrection of Jesus. The Gospel of Jesus is God's power to provide salvation for everyone who believes.

Life Example

We've already heard about some of Bill's actions under the influence of the drug, alcohol. Bill has a female counterpart whom we shall call Betty. Betty always considered herself a faithful wife and mother. She also considered herself to be a normal social drinker.

As the pressures of raising a family increased, Betty found that a drink now and then helped relieve some of her tension. It gave her a sense of well-being. It seemed to make her work easier. At least, so it seemed for a while.

As time went on, Betty needed to drink more often, and earlier in the day. She found herself sometimes falling asleep in the middle of the afternoon. At times, her husband found her asleep and sympathized with her when she explained about how much the work at home had increased, and how tired it made her. It never occurred to her that alcohol was in any way responsible for the changes taking place within her.

Finally, however, Betty found herself *needing* those drinks. She began to worry about the amount she was drinking. She also was praying to God to help her. She began to hide her supply of liquor. She had crossed over the invisible line of addiction and didn't know it.

Earlier we talked about insanity. How sane is it to hide bottles of booze in the toilet water tank? Normal people don't do such things. That isn't where we keep milk, or cans of soup, and it's not where bottles of beer or other drinks are kept either! But that's what Betty started doing. She had lots of hiding places. She feared running out of drinks.

Her prayers to God became desperate. She realized she was out of control. She could not *not* drink! She felt alone. She even began to feel deserted by God. "Why hasn't God answered my prayers?" she asked again and again. Betty didn't realize that God was already answering her prayers. God was allowing Betty to reach her "rock bottom," her point of desperation where she would cry out for help.

Eventually that day came and, through the loving care of family, friends, and professional help, Betty was led through a program of recovery. Betty now turned to God, truly believing that he was indeed able to restore her to sanity. More than that, God would use Betty as a power of example to give hope to others suffering from her problem. She learned forgiveness and acceptance, and, in doing so, she also learned to be forgiving and accepting. Just as Christ's cross had no strings attached to it, so Betty learned to love unconditionally.

Scripture Study

Psalm 46, Ephesians 2:18-32

Personal Meditations:

Evening Devotion

Prayer

O Holy Spirit, who not only has drawn me to faith, but who also keeps me in faith, thank you for your sustaining power which has kept me close to God this day. Each day is a time of testing, and I would have surely fallen were it not for your abiding presence. Thank you for returning me to your Word, through which you speak your words of encouragement and direction. Now may I rest in renewing sleep this night as your angels watch over me. Amen

Meditation

All too many of us take our Christian faith for granted. We who have suffered the effects of alcoholism know as few others do how tender that faith can be. How quickly we had our doubts and, in the midst of despair, even cursed God. Yet out of the furnace of affliction we found that though we were the unfaithful, God was faithful. We also found that while we concentrated on ourselves, we drifted farther from our God. When we ceased our complaints and began to turn back to him, we found him to be a willing listener who, indeed, answered our prayers. We began to understand what God meant when he told us that he would never leave us nor forsake us.

Our troubles really began when we thought more of ourselves than we should have. Our troubles started to dissolve when we began to give God the glory for our lives. Think of the disciples of Jesus. When Jesus was crucified and buried, what happened to the disciples? They ended up in fear and hiding. The promises of his resurrection and return to them seemed so impossible to accept. Simply because they could not see him any longer, they concluded he could no longer help them.

When Jesus rose and appeared to them alive in the flesh, they found they, indeed, had not been forsaken. Then, later, in his ascension, it seemed as if there was another abandonment, but the Spirit and power that Jesus had given them before his departure became fully operational on Pentecost. That same power is ours today in the Gospel. The Gospel of Jesus Christ reveals that Power greater than ourselves that can, indeed, restore us to sanity, and much more.

Life Example

We've seen some examples from the lives of "Bill" and "Betty" that showed some of the effects of alcohol. I would now like to have you meet another "Bill." This Bill began his drinking at an early age. He married early. That marriage ended in divorce because his wife could not stand Bill's way of living when he drank. Bill blamed her, not himself, for the divorce.

Within a few years Bill again married. This marriage also ended in divorce. Again Bill married, and another divorce. By this time, friends were trying to tell Bill that his drinking was the problem, but Bill wouldn't listen. Bill married a fourth time, and in a drunken rage, he grabbed a kitchen knife and stabbed his wife to death. Bill was sent to prison.

While in prison, Bill was introduced to a program of recovery from alcoholism. He finally understood that it was alcohol that had robbed him of his sanity, his marriages, and had made him a murderer. He had to accept responsibility for his actions and his crime. But God had not forsaken Bill. God saw to it that Bill received a parole from prison.

Today Bill is a successful businessman. He has a loving wife and family. You may not believe it, but his former wives and children from those marriages now love and accept him also. Bill found God's grace to be sufficient for every trouble and time of need. Bill learned what it is to be forgiven and to forgive, to be accepted and to accept. Bill learned the comfort of a Higher Power, his God and Savior.

Scripture Study

John 15:5, Ephesians 2:1-10

Personal Meditations:

Third Day

Morning Devotion

Prayer

Gracious Father, thank you for the gift of another day. Gracious Savior, thank you for redeeming my soul in order to reflect your glory in my life. Gracious Holy Spirit, thank you for recreating me in the image of Jesus and giving me new life. O blessed Trinity, may this day be one in which my will may be serving your most holy will. Into your care I entrust my body and soul and all things. Amen

Meditation

The third step of recovery says that we made a decision to turn our will and our life over to the care of God as we understood him. It is at this point that many Christians have great difficulty. Let's consider the problem one part at a time.

To make a decision was the hardest thing for an alcoholic to do. Alcohol is a drug that anesthetizes the mind and will, making it almost impossible for the affected person to make decisions of even the simplest nature. For that reason families of alcoholics find themselves taking over more and more of the alcoholic's responsibilities. This is a major mistake on their part, for it simply enables the alcoholic to continue on his path of self-destruction without having to be concerned about anything else.

The will of the alcoholic has been so affected by the drug that it cannot function normally. Chemical alcohol and chemical ether differ only by the factor of $H \pm O$, simple water. In other words, alcohol is liquid ether. The alcoholic, under the influence, is no more capable of making rational decisions of the will than is a person under anesthesia on an operating table.

The alcoholic Christian knew when he was drinking too much, but was unable to make the decision to stop. He knew he was offending God, but was unable to turn back from his sin. Friends and family may have told him to "be a man," "exercise some will power," "if you really loved us you would stop." He knew God's commands about overindulgence and could not properly respond to them. His will was destroyed.

Alcohol kept telling him, however, that he was in control. In response to the pleas of family and friends he would reply, "I'm all right, I can stop when I want to, I know my limits, I can take care of myself." I, I, I. The Christian had crossed over the line of addiction and his ego, fed by alcohol, felt it knew more than God or any other man what to do and how to do it.

When the Christian enters into a recovery program and reaches this step, it is quite an experience. After being subservient to alcohol for some time, the ability to make a decision is exhilarating and fearsome. Too many decisions made while drinking turned out to be disastrous.

However, now we are talking about turning our wills and lives over to the care of God. Here our baptismal grace really begins to shine in all its glory. The same Holy Spirit who touched our hearts then and has continued to abide with us, even when we were often ignorant of his presence, now enables us to truly — in faith — make a God-pleasing decision. We need to have the confidence that the decision can be made, by the grace of God.

Finally, we Christians have the tremendous advantage over other alcoholics in that we know who our God is. The God of our understanding is the God of revelation. He has revealed himself in his Word and in the Word made flesh, our Savior Jesus Christ. We are entrusting our wills and lives to the care of one who has shown his ultimate concern for us in his self-sacrifice on the cross. We have the joyous privilege of being able to continually search him out in the Scriptures for they "testify of me," Jesus said.

Life Example

It had been a long time since Bill had made any real life decisions. For years the daily decisions had been made by other members of his family. He had forgotten what responsibilities were.

Now that Bill had been to a detox treatment center and a rehabilitation program, he was working his way through the steps of recovery. When he came to this third step, he became terribly frightened. His family encouraged him, and his sponsors did likewise. However, he was still afraid to make a decision. He was afraid of failure again. He had broken so many promises in recent years, and he didn't want to set himself up for another setback.

Bill had almost lost his wife and family by his failures to keep his word while drinking. They felt he didn't care for them any more, when all the time he did care but was trapped by the drug. Now he didn't want to lose what little he had gained.

Finally, Bill was encouraged to speak with a clergyman who understood alcoholism. This, too, frightened him, but he was willing to give it a try. It took some time, but at last Bill was able to see that God's grace was indeed at work in his life. For the first time, he really began to understand the power that was available to him in the Gospel. He was thrilled to realize that God had never turned his back on him, but was really the instrument of his recovery. He learned to know the presence of the Holy Spirit and the direction that Spirit was ready to give to his life. Now, instead of his decision being one of his own making, and therefore a fearful one, his decision could be a faith-filled one, and therefore a strengthening one.

Bill felt a great weight lifted from his soul as his life was turned over to the care of God.

Scripture Study

Matthew 6:25-26, Matthew 7:7-8

Personal Meditations:

Evening Devotion

Prayer

Gracious Father, thank you for all your blessings of this day. Especially do I thank you for the blessing of your holy will and care for my body and soul. For so long I thought myself alone, but now I know how much you have been concerned about me. Thank you for cleansing me of my self-centeredness and opening to me your Spirit's directions for my life. May you continue to watch over me this night and grant me blessed rest. Amen

Meditation

In the course of recovery we learn a number of slogans. "Easy does it," and "One day at a time" are some of the first ones. Then comes "Let go, let God," which is a handy way of remembering this third step of recovery.

Letting go is the name of the game. Another way of describing our sinful nature is to picture it in terms of hanging on to temptations and sins. Some of our faults have been with us so long that we don't know what life would be like without them. Even though we may abhor what we became through alcohol, we are just as afraid to face life any differently. It's like the grip a person has on an electrical wire with the power on. The mind tells us it's killing us, yet we can't let go.

Step two reminded us of God's grace in our lives. In this third step, faith in that grace gives us new direction. Saint Paul said that through faith we are able to turn from the sin, and turn to God. That change of direction is the essence of repentance.

Concentration on the past, dwelling on the past sins, is

devastating to our life. God's grace in Jesus Christ has provided the atoning cover for all that. Repentance lays hold of that atonement. Now we can leave the past and turn to the future, one day at a time.

This day has been an eventful one. It marks a turning point in our recovery. We're no longer going it alone. Now we are indeed partners with God. Our sins have been laid at the foot of the cross, and we have taken up our own cross and are now following the Christ. Our wills and our lives are turned over to his blessed care. He will not let us down.

Life Example

Bill had been to a number of Alcoholics Anonymous meetings and was working his way through the third step. Many times at the meetings he heard about God and a higher power. At the same time he was told that Alcoholics Anonymous was not a religious organization, but rather a spiritual one. This language confused him. How could you talk about spirituality without talking about religion?

The answer, he found, was that *you* can't, but that Alcoholics Anonymous must. Though Alcoholics Anonymous speaks of God, it is not the objective of Alcoholics Anonymous to define God. Bill was told that the only purpose of Alcoholics Anonymous was to help you stay sober. Religious organizations have the task of defining God. Alcoholics Anonymous simply tells its people that God must be sought. It is up to the individual to do that seeking. It is up to the religious organizations to help the individual find the answers.

Bill found that he had to go back to his church to fill that religious void in his life. In order to turn his will and his life over to the care of God as he understood him, Bill had to seek answers about God. For the first time in his life Bill called the pastor with a sincere desire to find out more about God. Up until then, Bill had been coasting along with inadequate notions about the teachings of his church. Bill had never taken the Bible seriously. Bill realized he was spiritually impoverished!

When Bill met with his pastor, he discovered that the pastor was both informed about alcoholism and compassionate towards his needs. His pastor arranged for Bill to begin a series of meetings where he and the pastor could review the basic scriptural truths. Then he began a serious study of how these truths applied to his circumstances. A whole new world of God's revelation opened up to Bill. Bill had never thought he could get excited about God, but now he was.

Scripture Study

2 Timothy 3:10-17, Ephesians 3:14-21

Personal Meditations:

Fourth Day

Morning Devotion

Prayer

I thank you, heavenly Father, for graciously keeping me in your care this past night. In this new day give me the opportunity to live my life anew. I need not drag in the thoughts of the past, nor need I fear the future. By the power of the Holy Spirit enable me to live this day in such a way as to honor your name and magnify your glory. To that end bless this day through Christ my Lord and Savior. Amen

Meditation

Step Four of A.A.'s Twelve Step program says, "Made a searching and fearless moral inventory of ourselves." This step has often become a stumbling block for some. Remember, however, that with lives and wills turned over to God's care, our fears are offset by God's tender grace and mercy. The fourth step is no longer done within the shadow of judgment, but rather under the protection of forgiveness.

The Cross of Jesus "towers over wrecks of time" according to the words of the old gospel song. Through Christ, the Christian can look back over his life, painful as that may be, with a sense of victory over the past. For the Christian, the inventory begins with prayer to God asking for the courage to make the inventory, as well as for the wisdom to search with understanding. God casts out the fear of the inventory. Its purpose is to pinpoint areas that need further examination and to set new directions for the future.

It is important for us to remember that a drug is

impersonal. It has no motives, it has no purposes, it is simply a chemical. We cannot blame a drug for moral problems, nor can we credit a drug for accomplishments. As the inventory search begins, we must go back to times before any drug was involved. Here the honesty of our search will begin to show itself. There were character defects and assets present before alcohol became a part of our lives. We were also in a relationship with God at that time, whatever that relationship may have been!

As the inventory continues, we find that some of the things we were blaming on alcohol were really present before our drinking, though maybe to a different degree. Alcohol does not create characteristics: it can only reduce or enhance them. If we turned from God during our drinking, perhaps there were already seeds of doubt and distrust present before our drinking. If we lost our sense of self-worth while drinking, perhaps there were signs of inferiority before our drinking. If we felt more courageous when we drank, perhaps we were already strong of spirit before we drank. These and many other items become part of the inventory checklist.

Our involvement with our church has to be honestly examined as well. Certainly we no longer felt like a part of the congregational fellowship when we were under the influence. But how well integrated were we in the body of Christ before we ever drank at all? Were we asking a feeble faith to sustain us in the midst of great pressures? How familiar were we with God's precious Word which, with the sacraments, are God's means of sharing with us his grace? To what extent were we involved in prayer and meditation? To what extent did we really rely on God, especially the strength offered our souls through the body and blood of Christ our Lord?

While drinking, where did we turn for help? To God? To our drinking buddies? Who were our friends? Fellow members of the fellowship of believers? Friends whose only common denominator was a bottle? On and on the inventory continues, as it really must if we are to get an honest picture of ourselves, past and present.

Life Example

When Bill felt ready to take his fourth step, he really didn't know what to do. He was not thrilled with the idea of digging through the pain of the past. On the other hand, he knew there were lots of loose ends from the past that needed attention. Finally, he turned to his sponsor. Bill had found a Christian friend in Alcoholics Anonymous who had consented to be his sponsor. And he found that for Christians, it is a considerable advantage to have a sponsor who is also Christian. He had to have someone who had walked his way ahead of him to be an example for his own steps.

Bill's sponsor sat down with him and first shared his own experiences with his faith. He told how much he had had to relearn the basic doctrines of the Scriptures. He'd had to find a renewed view of sin and grace, Law and Gospel, Word and Sacrament, self and church, etc. Most importantly, he had had to relearn the real joy of redemption through Christ and what that meant for him as he looked at his life, past and present.

From this conversation Bill was better prepared to begin his fourth step. Bill's sponsor also suggested to Bill that he write down his inventory. That way he would have a better opportunity to sit down with his sponsor for review, especially if there were questions to talk about.

Another thing his sponsor told Bill was to not only write down the bad, but also the good. Alcohol sometimes robs people of the view of the good times. In the self-pity brought on by the drug, some of the good qualities are overlooked. It was suggested that Bill start with two columns on the paper. For every "bad" item listed he should try to think of a "good" item.

As Bill began in this fashion, he found that there were many blessings from God for which he could be grateful. He found that, in spite of the tough times, there were also times when he felt good, when he was grateful to have others, whom God placed around him, who preserved him from total self-destruction. He found he had enjoyed outings with the family. He had still been productive at work. He began to see that his inventory needn't be all negative. The inventory that Bill formerly feared turned out to be a blessing.

Scripture Study

Job 13:13 (look at context), Psalm 139:1-5

Personal Meditations:

Evening Devotion

Prayer

Dear God, what a day this has been! Having thought about so many things of the past, and having realized your providence all the days of my life, how differently I viewed today. My heart is filled to overflowing with my feelings toward you. In the past I took you so for granted. Today I felt you by my side. Thank you for this gift of knowing you in the fullness of your love for me through Jesus Christ. I am able to rest this night assured of your continued care. Amen

Meditation

A fearless inventory that searches through our lives does indeed help us become more honest with ourselves. We find that our alcoholic view of the past was considerably different from reality. As a matter of fact, when we come to step ten, we shall find that it is necessary to continually revise our view of both past and present as we learn more about our disease and about ourselves.

We have also begun to realize that though the task of recovery is tremendous, nevertheless it is made easier by breaking the task down into these steps. One day at a time, one step at a time, we progress. Have you ever considered why the almighty Creator God chose to take six days to make this universe? This was not for his benefit, but for ours. God set for us a pattern for living. The more we reduce the tasks of our lives into workable units, the greater will be our sense of accomplishment and the less our frustration.

The first time we approach an inventory of ourselves there are roadblocks besides fear. Our minds have been affected by alcohol. Emotional detoxification can extend over a period of a year, or two, or more! Until we are completely free of the longer-lasting effects of alcohol, our view of ourselves, including our past, is clouded. We'll have more to say on this when we get to step ten.

Step four helps us to place our lives back into the perspective of community — both secular and sacred. Drinking causes us to withdraw from society and turn within. God's grace in the healing blood of Jesus motivates us to reach out beyond ourselves. Our inventory helps to clarify what alcohol did to us in robbing us of our place in fellowship with others. We must learn now to replace the "I" with "we."

Life Example

There are two basic types of Bettys. On the one hand, there is Betty who began as a social drinker and progressed to socializing in every bar and party she could find. If anyone said they were going to have a drink, she would say, "So shall I."

On the other hand, there is the Betty who became more withdrawn as her drinking progressed. This Betty finally became a prisoner within her own bedroom. Her only "friend" was her bottle. All other social contacts were shut off.

The first Betty often found herself waking up in strange places with strangers by her side. She found she no longer had any control over her moral life. She would do anything with anybody for another drink. Often she had no idea what had happened or when.

The second Betty simply had her life shut down. Even her husband and children could not reach her. She had put everything out of her life except alcohol. Finally the drinking no longer gave her any satisfaction. She simply became more withdrawn and alone within herself.

Both Bettys were getting sicker and sicker. Eventually, both reached the point where all systems shut down, and they were simply sick and tired of being sick and tired. They both found hope in their recovery, and when they came to this fourth step something happened.

Though the drinking lifestyles of these Bettys were so different, their inventories were amazingly similar with regard to feelings and the progression of the disease of alcoholism. Both had to rejoice in the fact that God had redeemed them through Christ, not only from their sins, but also from their alcoholic view of life itself.

They were pointed in the direction of fellowship with Christ, and also fellowship with their Christian community, once more. In the context of that Christian community they were ready to take the further steps necessary for their recovery.

Scripture Study

Galations 5:16-26

Personal Meditations:

Fifth Day

Morning Devotion

Prayer

Gracious Father in heaven, you have brought me to the beginning of another day. I am grateful for your protection this past night. Be with me, I pray, in all that I do that my words and actions might be pleasing to you. Guide me in seeking out ways in which to better serve you that my life may glorify your holy name. Through Christ my Lord, I pray. Amen

Meditation

The fifth step of the Alcoholics Anonymous program says that we admitted to God, to ourselves, and to another fellow human being the exact nature of our wrongs. Up until now our steps have been private, for even in step four the involvement of our sponsor was only a suggestion. Now another person must become involved. The Christian parallel is the act of confession.

Many of us hesitate to involve anyone else in the process of confession. We feel that it is a private matter between us and our God. So it is, but it is not only so! Our Lord himself commands us to involve other members of the body of Christ when, in the Book of James, he tells us we are to confess our sins to each other and to pray for each other.

The big question, of course, is how is this done? The answer begins with finding someone who is both trustworthy and who has some understanding of alcoholism, and who is in the fellowship of the church. It could be that we do not know any such person. Then we must ask. This step is so important that it must not be rushed. Take the time to find the right person with whom to share your story.

Here I must put in a plug for our professional clergy. At one time it may have been hard to find a clergyperson well versed in alcoholism, because that was not a part of their training. Today, however, great strides have been taken in this area. If your particular clergyperson is uncomfortable in dealing with this subject, perhaps he or she knows someone to whom you may be referred.

Next, we set aside enough time so that we are not hurried. We arrange to meet our friend and bring along with us our fourth step inventory. It is important that we begin with prayer, asking God to strengthen us and to guide us. It is also important to remember that it is not necessary to share everything, only that which we wish to share at that time.

As we begin to share our past with another person, we are really bringing into the light those things we've kept in darkness far too long. This sharing experience draws us into an opportunity to bear one another's burdens, and so fulfill the law of Christ. As we finally unburden ourselves of the weight that we have carried for so long, we find that we are relieved and lifted up.

Our friend first will be a good listener. Next, our friend will share with us some words of comfort and encouragement. She will remind us that Christians are sinners and saints at the same time. We have been reconciled to the Father by grace through the merits of Jesus. Our sins are covered by the atoning blood of Christ. They can haunt us no more.

We usually will find that this step opens doors to new paths for us to explore. Freed from the weight of the past, we can now begin moving forward with new energy and zeal. This fifth step marks a major achievement in our growth.

Life Example

Bill had talked a lot during his drinking days, and he had talked with lots of people. None of that talk, however, was very revealing of his true feelings. His tongue was in gear, but his mind wasn't. Now, as Bill prepared to take his fifth step, he realized that, for the first time in his life, he had to be honest and open, not only with God, but with a fellow human being.

Bill had spoken about taking his fifth step with several good friends and finally came to a decision about which person was to share his experience. It so happened that it was a clergyman of the Christian faith, but not of the same church that Bill belonged to. This particular clergyman was also a recovering alcoholic and knew what Bill was going through.

Bill and "Father Pat" met one morning and began their session with prayer. Then under the grace of God, and with a mutual trust in their Savior Jesus Christ, the fifth step continued. Bill shared with Father Pat his fourth step inventory while Father Pat simply listened. When Bill was finished, he was told to throw the papers away. This was a simple act that symbolized that all his past sins had been washed in the blood of the Lamb. Bill no longer had to consider them a burden.

Bill was led to a greater appreciation of the great biblical teachings and Law and Gospel, justification and sanctification, sin and grace. For years Bill had misunderstood how God's grace worked. He had thought of God as a great judge expecting Bill to perform to perfection. The more Bill became involved with alcohol, the farther from God he felt himself to be. He felt there was no way to find God's approval any more.

Bill was led to see that our Father in heaven is indeed full of wrath over our sins. But he was also led to see that God no longer looks at our sins, because he first sees the sacrifice of Jesus which covers them. Bill began to see that righteousness, being right with God, was God's gift to him through Jesus Christ. Righteousness of Christ is like a coat that we wear to cover our unrighteousness.

Then, step by step, Father Pat encouraged Bill to look at the parts of his inventory where he had found evidence of God's continuing blessings in his life. Building on these with a sense of true gratitude, Bill would be able to set new directions for his life. The important thing for Bill was that he had finally laid his life on the table for God to go to work on. No more hiding, no more rationalizing, no more fear. Bill felt a great sense of relief.

Scripture Study

Psalm 32:5, Titus 3:3-7

Personal Meditations:

Evening Devotion

Prayer

Lord Jesus Christ, you have blessed me with new freedom this day. For the first time in years I have been able to look at friends and family face to face without feelings of inner guilt and fear. Having finally dealt with the sins of my past, hidden within for all too long, I have been able to really experience the love and friendship of those near and dear to me. Thank you for this wonderful gift of experiencing your forgiveness. Send your holy angels to watch over me this night. Into your hands I commend myself. Amen

Meditation

In the past, while drinking, we didn't face our short-comings or failures. We were quick to blame everything else and everyone else for what went wrong in our lives. Now, however, we have learned to take all this past to the cross of Christ. Christ leads us to confession of our sins, and from that confession to freedom and a new-found strength.

We don't ever have to go back to what we once were. Even more important, we can now go on to what God already declares us to be through Christ. Isn't that something! All through the years we were trying to prove ourselves to God and man. We no longer have to "prove" anything to anybody.

step. We become restored to a respected place in the families of our home, our community, our church. Alcohol had put us into isolation. These steps of recovery have moved us out of that prison. In the opening up of ourselves to God and another fellow human being, we broke out of that self-inflicted bondage into a freedom to be shared with others.

We no longer fear others. We see others as fellow redeemed friends. Reconciliation now extends into our relationships with other people. The potential for our returning to functional honesty has been translated into action. This is a precious advance in our recovery.

This freedom to be honest enables us to deal with people in a way that sometimes surprises us. We now wonder at all the time and energy we wasted in the rationalizations, the connings, the excuses, and all the other mental gymnastics that we went through while drinking.

We're now ready to take another step.

Life Example

Bill now began to look at people differently. He finally saw his wife as one who really did love him after all. During the drinking years, he had felt she was nothing but a critic and a nag. Now he saw that whatever she had said and done was in reaction to his drinking. She had become disillusioned and bitter as Bill's drinking affected her life. It would take some time for the healings to take place, but Bill knew now that a beginning had been made.

Bill began to see that all those people he thought were his enemies were really his friends whom he had alienated. Soon he would learn to make amends to them wherever possible. Bill started to reach out to people around him and found that they welcomed him.

Bill was very fearful about becoming involved with his church again. What would people say? Would they be talking about him behind his back? He finally called the pastor who, fortunately, knew about alcoholism and its effects on the lives of people, and Bill was assured that most of his fears were unfounded. Should there be someone who said something unkind to him — and that possibility always exists — Bill would have to deal with it by the same forgiveness he had learned to know in his fifth step.

Bill took his pastor's advice and is now an active and involved member of his parish. A person not knowing Bill's background would never guess what a transformation had taken place.

Now there remained the problem of what to do with the shortcomings revealed and confessed in steps four and five. There are still more steps to take, but the journey is becoming smoother, and Bill's reliance on God's grace becomes stronger.

Scripture Study

Romans 3:21-28, 5:12-21

Personal Meditations:

Sixth Day

Morning Devotion

Prayer

O Holy Spirit, this day begins a new part of my life. I have looked at my past and have found much that must be renewed. There is much that needs to be changed. I am helpless to do so. I need to have your power at work in my heart to renew in me a right spirit and to cleanse me from my past. Be with me this day, I pray, as I begin. Through Christ my Lord and blessed Savior I pray. Amen

Meditation

Alcoholics Anonymous' sixth step of recovery states that we were entirely ready to have God remove all these defects of character. The seventh step says that we humbly asked him to remove our shortcomings. We notice that one step deals with attitude and the other with action. Right now we concentrate on our attitude about our defects of character, our sins.

It's one thing to take an inventory and to make a confession of our sins. It's an entirely different matter to start doing something about our character defects and begin to change them. Old habits are deeply imbedded. Old ways are hard to change. The first thing we must do is see ourselves as really ready to have something happen.

Most of our character defects have been with us a long time. They didn't just suddenly appear on the scene. Many of them were with us even before alcohol took control of our lives. Our fourth and fifth steps showed us how very deeply rooted our sins have been.

We've started on a journey which is taking us away from our evil past and on toward God. Repentance is a turning process. It isn't instantaneous. It does take time, and it does have a definite pattern. With the acknowledgment of our sins and sorrow over them (contrition), and with our sharing of our past with another (confession), we have come to a crossroads. We could stop here and be relatively safe. To proceed is somewhat threatening. Why? Because it means giving up something.

Old sins have a way of becoming old friends as well as enemies. Simply because they've been with us so long, we are not sure how our lives will be without them. Our character defects have actually defined our lives and our identities, so much so that we are not at all sure how we will be without them. Yet, we must move on if our repentance is to be genuine.

One question we must ask ourselves at this point is this — do I want my future life to be the same as my past? If we desire our lives to be different, we must let go of those things that have caused us so much harm. Here is where the power of God's grace and love is necessary. Only God is able to remove our character defects. We cannot do it. Our own reason and strength have been so warped by sin that we are incapable of restoring ourselves. In this sixth step we turn to our merciful God and ask him to remove our defects of character.

Life Example

When Bill first came to a program of recovery, he had been living a rather wild life. He had been involved with several gangs. He had, in his words, broken every law and then some. Even his appearance was something to behold. He was dressed in greasy, well-worn work clothes. His beard reached halfway down his chest and his hair fell the same distance down his back. He was scarred and tattooed, and bore the signs of many brawls. Some who met him weren't sure he was going to make it in the program of recovery.

And Bill didn't really want to be in the program. He was given a choice by the judge: either he went for treatment for his alcoholism or he went to jail. It was that simple. Bill chose treatment as the lesser of two evils.

As time went on, however, Bill began to listen to what was being said to him. He found others who had begun like he had and made it. He began to consider another way of life as being possible, even though for years the only words he had heard were, "You'll never amount to anything."

Today, people who know Bill would never think he could have been like he once was. The major change began when Bill trusted God enough to think that he could remove his defects of character. Bill had never really thought change was either needed or possible. Now he wanted desperately to change. He had to think about what he was told about sin.

"Though your sins be as scarlet they shall be as white as snow," Isaiah said long ago. Such radical change is not only possible, it is the reality of God's grace, through the merits of Jesus Christ, that gave hope to Bill. The more he became friends with other people and heard them share with him the changes that God had worked in their lives, the more Bill became convinced that his character defects, his sins, could be dealt with also. Bill was ready to consider the possibilities of a new way of life.

Scripture Study

Psalm 51:10, Colossians 1:21-22

Personal Meditations:

Evening Devotion

Prayer

Gracious and merciful God, this day has also been a new experience for me. I must thank you for enabling me to see those around me in a new light, the light of your forgiveness. As I recognize the logs in my own eyes, I am more able to accept the little slivers in the eyes of others. Now may your Spirit be with me this night. May your Word continue to dwell in me richly. May the love of Jesus continue to find a home in my heart. Amen

Meditation

A question we often ask ourselves at this point is why did we hang on to so many character defects, so many sins? Though the answer is complex, may we suggest that one of the reasons was that it made it easier for us to carry on the life we chose to live.

Take, for example, pride. As long as we clung to pride, we could say to ourselves that we were better than others. We could pick on their faults and overlook our own. We could justify for ourselves our many sinful actions. We could avoid being really honest with ourselves. Of course we didn't have to face God, because we were perfect — or so we thought.

Or consider envy. We could work ourselves into a good pity party, the "poor me's" being jealous of what others had that we didn't. We could then justify another drink to either run from the truth or to bolster ourselves for another day. Either way, it was self-destructive.

On and on the list could go. Each sin, each fault, we could twist and turn to our own advantage. The further down the road to alcoholism we went, the easier such thinking became. We just about rationalized ourselves into the grave.

Now, having been shown the inevitable course of our actions and the real destructive force of our sins, we are able to say we are ready to have God remove these defects. We now want a different kind of life. For the first time in many years we have hope for something better than we have had.

Life Example

Betty had blamed her husband and children for just about everything that had gone wrong in her life. If it weren't for the children, she could have gone on with her schooling and would now be a career woman with status in the community. If her husband would support her more, she wouldn't have such feelings of emptiness. If her husband would just get home at a decent hour, she wouldn't have had that affair with the neighbor.

Betty's whole world was wrapped up in "if's." Not once did Betty consider that some of her problems might be due to something within herself. Never once did Betty consider that the defects of character, the sins she was nurturing within, had anything to do with her troubles. She transferred the blame outside of herself, and used her problems as a reason to run to the bottle for solace and escape.

When Betty took her fourth step inventory, she was truly shocked at what she discovered about herself. She really was amazed that her husband had stood by her so long. After taking her fifth step she was now ready to let God remove her defects of character. For the first time in her life she began to think in terms of repentance and renewal. Betty had finally taken ownership and responsibility for herself.

Betty thought back to the times she had prayed to God to help her stop drinking. She thought back to the bitterness she had felt when it seemed as if God was not listening to her. Now she realized that it was not God who had not been listening. Betty's prayers had been quite conditional. She had indeed been asking God to help her stop drinking, but she had reserved her sins for herself to deal with. She hadn't really had any desire at that time for God to get too deeply involved in her life. Now she was ready for changes to be made. Seeing the potential of a full and rich Christian life gave her hope.

Scripture Study

Psalm 32:10, Psalm 131, 2 Thessalonians 3:3

Personal Meditations:

Seventh Day

Morning Devotion

Prayer

Almighty and merciful Father, thank you for another day in which to grow in your grace. This is the day I am to ask you to remove my shortcomings. Set aside my anxious thoughts and my fears. Help me to anticipate with eagerness and joy the person you wish me to be. No matter how much my sins have been a part of my life, cast them far from me so that I may grow in faith and trust in you. In the name of Christ my loving Savior I pray. Amen

Meditation

As we saw, the sixth step of recovery involved a change in attitude. Now the seventh step involves action in that it humbly asks God to remove our shortcomings. As with the fourth and fifth steps, it would be far easier to remain at our current level of attitude than to move on to action. To take this seventh step is to make a commitment to God.

We've said that many old sins become comfortable to live with. These sins play their parts in developing our characters and personalities. In short, they are involved with our identities. When we ask God to remove sins, we are risking a change in our identities. That also involves us in risking our relationships with others.

"Birds of a feather . . ." So goes the old saying. Have you ever stopped to consider just how different relationships were formed during the drinking days? "Drinking buddies" were only buddies as long as they thought it could be to their advantage. When you really needed help, where were they? If you had drinks available, they were there, but when else? By the same token, why did you choose to be with them, except for the simple fact they could provide you with a drink? What else did you have in common?

What is our personality going to be like after the short-comings are removed? How shall we establish new relationships? These and many others are the questions with which we shall now have to deal.

Let's not forget just what is going on, however. We are asking God to do the removing of the sins and character defects. God is the one who will be in charge of our lives. Here is where our trust in God begins to meet its test. In asking God to remove our character defects, we are saying to God that we are going to quit trying to shape our lives by ourselves. God is no longer going to be kept out of our lives by our stubborn resistance.

How is God going to remove these defects? God chooses to use some very special tools. At first glance they don't look like much to mankind. Some water, some words, some bread, some wine. Touched by God's special grace, however, these very common and mundane elements become instruments of mercy. They are the channels through which the Holy Spirit leads us to the cross of Christ, and works in us the forgiveness of sins, faith, and new life.

Our commitment, therefore, to step seven is also a commitment to renewed spiritual activity. It means for us a return to God's Word, the Bible. It means for us a renewing of our baptismal commitment. It means for us a faithfulness at worship and the Lord's Supper. Only through these means of grace can the cleansing take place within us.

Life Example

The Bill we meet this time is somewhat different from the others so far. Bill and his wife both drank a lot, and both qualified as alcoholics. By God's grace both entered into programs of recovery. Many people thought that the two of them would now make a marvelous couple as sober, thankful people. Sad to say, such was not to be the case at all.

You see, Bill met and married his wife when both were already alcoholics. The qualities which led them to each other were highly affected by the drug. Simply put, they each married someone who was functioning artificially in life.

When Bill and his wife began to sober up and work through their programs of recovery, they each began to change. At first, they thought this would be wonderful. However, their rate of recovery was not the same. Also, when they began to work these sixth and seventh steps, something else happened to their relationship.

Bill's wife discovered that the real Bill beneath the surface of alcohol was a completely different man than she previously had experienced. The same held true for Bill and his view of his wife. As time went on they found that they were really strangers to each other.

Bill tried desperately to continue in his love for his wife. He prayed that she and he could grow together in their new life under God's grace. However, his wife could not accept the changes that were taking place. She still desired the high-rolling life of before, sober or not. She finally filed for a divorce.

Bill's heart was broken. He struggled for reconciliation. He sought counseling from both his pastor and a professional marriage counselor. But his wife refused all efforts to save the marriage. It would have been quite easy for Bill to have fallen into an alcoholic relapse. He prayed to God for strength not to do that.

The divorce became final, and Bill found himself alone. But he was soon reminded that he was not really alone. He not only had his God with him, but also had many new friends in his church. It would take time, but Bill would perhaps also find a new helpmate.

Scripture Study

2 Corinthians 12:7-10

Personal Meditations:

Evening Devotion

Prayer

Dear God, resolving to work on the new person and cast out the old is not easy. There are so many temptations to fall back into old paths. I am grateful for your presence and your strength. Try as I will, I still slip and stumble. Thank you for your forgiveness in Christ Jesus my Lord. Help me to continue on my growth to genuine Christian maturity. Grant me peace of mind and body this night. In the name of Jesus I pray. Amen

Meditation

Changing life through the removal of defects of character is similar to a birth process. Both involve pain, but in the pain there is gain. Jesus said that, unless we are born of water and of the Spirit, we cannot enter into the Kingdom of God. The reference to Holy Baptism is obvious, but there is also that special comparison to birth. One, the birth of the flesh, is of human origin. It is temporal in nature. It has a beginning and it has an end. The birth that involves the Spirit of God is of divine origin and is eternal in nature.

Regardless of how this birth is described — born again, born anew, or born from above — it is a birth arranged and managed by God himself. It moves our lives into the dimensions of the spiritual. We now begin living by more than just human appetites and desires. This is what Jesus meant when he said that man does not live by bread alone. The Christian lives by the Word of God. "For me to live is Christ," is the famous apostolic claim.

As God removes the sins and character defects of the Christian alcoholic, we find a new person emerging in the genuine Christian tradition of a regenerated soul. There is literally no limit to the potential of such a person. The more free he is of the bondage of his past, the more able he is to produce wonders in the Kingdom of God on earth.

It has been our experience that the recovering alcoholic Christians are often the most grateful and most productive members of our congregations. Perhaps only those who have experienced the hellish horrors of the slide into alcoholism can truly appreciate God's rescue and gift of new life.

Life Example

Bill and his wife (another couple this time) were divorced while he was drinking. His wife felt forced into the divorce as the only way to protect their children and her sanity. We are not in the position to judge her decision at that time. Bill did not oppose the divorce. At the time, he saw it as giving him more freedom to continue in the habits that were leading to his self-destruction.

Bill's wife had joined a support group for families of suffering alcoholics. Through their help and through the counsel of Christian friends, she maintained her contact with Bill, and, deep down inside her heart, her love for him as well.

It took years, but Bill did finally enter into a program of recovery. As he started to work his steps, he began to see how much he needed to bear the responsibility for the failure of his marriage. He and his former wife reestablished contact and began looking back over the years together.

They also sought the counsel of a Christian minister who helped them to realize how much their lives had been destroyed by chemical alcohol. Now, as the sins of the past become covered with the blood of Christ, as the defects are removed by God's Spirit through the means of grace, a whole new relationship can be developed. This wouldn't happen overnight, but it could happen.

Bill and his former wife worked and prayed together. They had many talks. They sought much counsel. I'm happy to say that they discovered that God was leading them to a deeper love than they had ever had before. They eventually chose to remarry. Their wedding took place with hundreds of members of Alcoholics Anonymous and Al-Anon as witnesses. Their Christian wedding also gave testimony to the power of God's grace in their lives.

Scripture Study

2 Corinthians 5:17-21

Personal Meditations:

Eighth Day

Morning Devotion

Prayer

Today is a special gift from you, O Lord, for I am convinced you are renewing me in spirit and in soul. How grateful I am that, in spite of my sins of the past, you have reached into my heart with your love. With the merits of my Savior Jesus I am able to stand before you. Grant me your Spirit's special guidance this day in all that I do. Amen

Meditation

Progress in recovery involves a sort of good news/bad news situation. The good news is that we are growing in grace and definitely improving. The bad news is that each step has more responsibilities attached to it. Thanks be to God who strengthens us in Jesus Christ!

The eighth step of recovery in Alcoholics Anonymous says that we made a list of all persons we had harmed, and became willing to make amends to them all. Here again is an attitude step. In step nine we shall be asked to actually make those amends wherever possible. For now, we begin by making a list.

At first this task may seem overwhelming. How can we possibly remember all those we have touched with our alcoholic sins? The truth is we can't. Furthermore, if we happened to have had alcoholic blackouts, there is no way we can recall whom we hurt during those blackouts. The list may also include those we harmed before alcohol even entered the picture. So what do we do?

We begin. The Chinese say that a thousand-mile journey begins with just one step. No one says that our list must be all-inclusive. Alcoholics tend to be perfectionists. Alcoholics also tend to be rationalists. When faced with problems these two qualities mix together and come up with this thought: Since I can't do a perfect job, I won't even start. No way! Remember, we've asked God to remove our character defects. He will remove this one too. We start our list by remembering anyone we have harmed, no matter who or when or how.

Once started, we continue to add to the list. As the list grows we feel the pain of the past. We become ever more aware of the sorrow we've caused in the lives of many. We also become more aware of the harm we did to ourselves.

From time to time we pause in our list-making to offer a silent prayer of thanks that God has redeemed us from such a life. We could have continued on until we either went insane or died. We were rescued and given life. We live the life of the risen Christ. What a joy!

Having completed our list, as far as possible for now, we turn to making a decision. Calling upon all the strength of our sanctified will, we become willing to make amends to all those whom we have hurt. This means a willingness to face the past directly. This means a resolve not to side-step people. It means taking ownership of matters for which we were responsible along with whatever costs may be involved. We said this was not an easy step.

Life Example

This particular Bill had spent a number of years bouncing from one detoxification center to another. He lost track of the times he had "dried out." He had even spent some time in a mental hospital because, as it often happens with alcoholics, he had been diagnosed as a manic depressive by an ill-informed physician.

He had also been talked into longer term rehabilitation, and had spent several terms in such facilities. After each of these experiences he had gone back to the bottle, sometimes also with the addition of prescription drugs, which he also abused.

Looking back on all this, Bill had absolutely no idea how many people he had harmed along the way. Now that he was in a recovery program that seemed to be really working, he didn't want to lose what he had gained. In desperation he turned to his sponsor for help. Bill's sponsor knew exactly what Bill's problem was. Bill was trying to do everything at once. He was trying to reach back to everyone in every place to make his list.

Bill's sponsor recognized that Bill also had a deep spiritual problem. He suggested that Bill contact his pastor. Bill asked his sponsor if he would go with him to see the pastor. Together they set up an appointment.

At the meeting, Bill was put at ease when the pastor who was familiar with such situations, told him that his fears and problems were not unique to him. Others had been there before Bill, and the solution was not as impossible as Bill had imagined.

Bill's pastor first reminded Bill that he was working on this step as a forgiven Christian. His relationship with God and his amends to God had already been taken care of through the sacrifice of Jesus. Then the pastor suggested that Bill use an old educational principle to solve his problem. Begin with the known and work to the unknown. It was suggested that Bill begin his list with those closest and dearest to him. From there he could start working backward as far as he cared to go. Furthermore, he shouldn't worry about how complete the list would be, for there would be another time when he would deal with this matter again.

Bill was much relieved when he heard this and went home to write down his list. This step didn't look so impossible anymore.

Scripture Study

Matthew 6:12, Philippians 2:1-5

Personal Meditations:

Evening Devotion

Prayer

Thank you, O God, for being with me this day. For the blessing of your Spirit and his gifts, I am grateful. For protection from temptation and deliverance from evil, I am grateful. For opportunities to express my love for you, I am grateful. For helping me to be willing to make amends to those I have harmed along my life's way, I am grateful. Be with me this night and let me rest in your watchful angel's care. Through Christ, my Savior, I pray. Amen

Meditation

Sometimes, when the eighth step is being worked, a person tries too hard to think of the harms done only when drinking. This is not what this step says. We are asked here to look back at our life and consider any persons we have harmed, period, not just through drinking. This relates to what we said before about character defects. There was harm being done to people before we ever began drinking.

If we are going to be truly repentant, we cannot limit our analysis of our lives in any way. It is an all or nothing situation. These steps, therefore, cannot be worked in a day. We cannot hurry them. Patience is a virtue for which we shall be praying all the time. Alcoholics are always trying to rush things. We must learn to slow down and work very methodically.

As we work on our list of persons, we take note of the particular harms that made us think of that person. Here again it is helpful to have paper and pencil handy and write these things down. Later we can throw our notes away, but for now they can be useful to our thinking.

Each person is going to awaken different emotions. It takes time for us to consider each situation. We want to clearly establish the specifics of our responsibility for the harms done. This will help us when we ask God's Spirit to guide us in shaping our wills to make amends to these persons. We will want to put ourselves in their position and empathize with them. This will help us to rid ourselves of the feelings of superiority which we once had, and which led us to the harm. Under the cover of the atonement we can identify with the hurt, and be more ready to heal the wounds of the past. We're now ready to move on to another step.

Life Example

Betty arrived at this step somewhat confused. Her drinking had all been done as a "closet drinker" and, therefore, she felt no harm had been done to anyone but herself. In public she always made certain that she was in "good condition," so no one would suspect her secret. Betty also lived alone and therefore had no family responsibilities.

The very fact that Betty at least recognized there was harm to herself was a beginning. Here is where her list had to begin. She was at the head of the list. The more Betty thought about that, the more she realized that she had also hurt the One who had made her. She had thought of herself in isolation for so long that she had even isolated herself from God. In so doing, she also insulated herself from feelings about God.

Now Betty realized that her harm to herself was indeed an offense to God, whose Spirit had claimed her body as his temple. She had desecrated the very thing that was supposed to be an instrument of worship and of glorifying God. The overpowering wonder of God's grace filtered into every nook and cranny of Betty's thoughts at this point.

Betty began also to realize the extent to which the cross

of Christ now reached into her life. She was now willing to make amends, but how to make amends to God? Answer: she couldn't do that. Any amends to God had already been made by the satisfaction of Jesus through his death. But Betty could now begin thinking of making amends to herself.

Furthermore, as Betty thought about all this, she discovered something else. She thought about all the persons with whom she came into contact each week. Sales persons, clerks, delivery persons, hairdresser, people at work, etc. Surely, her attitude toward all these must have been affected by her drinking. Her list now began to grow. Her resolve to make amends extended now beyond herself. Betty was growing.

Scripture Study

1 John 4:19-21

Personal Meditations:

Ninth Day

Morning Devotion

Prayer

Thank you, O God, for keeping me from all harm and danger while I slept this past night. This day I ask for the power of your spirit to enable me to begin making my amends to those people I have hurt in so many ways. I am afraid to begin, but I am confident that you can and will help me overcome my fear. For the sake of Jesus I pray. Amen

Meditation

The ninth step in recovery says to make direct amends to such people (people I had harmed), whenever possible, except when to do so would injure them or others. Several things are to be noted about this step. The word "direct" means that we do not make our amends through third parties. We are committed to direct encounters. The phrase "whenever possible" points out the fact that we are not required to begin an odyssey of searching out people of our past. As circumstances permit, we make such amends as are possible. "Except" underscores the fact that there are some things in the past that are best left alone. To "injure" implies that in some cases our attempts to heal old wounds may indeed cause more damage than if we had done nothing.

People have been known to confess all sorts of things and then go on living as though nothing had happened. Nothing changes in their lifestyle. That is false repentance. Faith that is genuine, as the book of James points out, shows itself in transformation of life. For the Christian alcoholic, this is a transformation step. Faith is tested as it is translated into action. Here is where we find out whether our trust in God is just so many words, or genuine confidence that God can truly change our lives.

Direct amends usually begin with those closest to us. Members of our own family were the first and most severely hurt by our addiction. Rightfully, they should be the first to feel the healing effects of recovery. Because alcoholism is a family disease, the members of the family have hurts whose scars run deep. The process of making amends to them may take some time. We ought not be discouraged if our attempts to make amends are met with some suspicion at first. In the past, we made so many promises and then broke them, that to accept more good words from us now is not easy. Patience is truly in order!

The possibility of making amends to some people has been taken away from us. Perhaps some have moved away and we no longer know where they are. We pray to meet them again some day. Others may have died. Here, there is pain as we regret not being able to make our amends. We turn once more to forgiveness from an understanding God through Jesus Christ.

Then there are instances where opportunity presents itself and we reach out to make our amends, but the offended people will have nothing more to do with us. We have hurt them so much that their fear of more hurt sets up an impenetrable wall. In that case, we must be satisfied with having made the overtures. We turn the matter over to God and pray that one day their reception of us will change.

Some memories of the past involve actions and circumstances that are best left in the past. It's possible that, though the person whom we directly harmed may not be further hurt, there now may be innocent people involved with that person who would be emotionally injured by our bringing up the past. To reach back into such memories would bring further harm to the persons involved. Here we must ask

God's Spirit to give us the wisdom to know when to do nothing.

Finally, there is the great joy brought about by settling hurts of the past. Reconciliation is just a word until translated into action through confession, forgiveness, and acceptance. As we become reconciled to persons we had harmed, we find the weights upon our souls being lifted, and our lives truly begin to find zeal and excitement.

Life Example

Bill's past was a confused and complicated one. Bill was a bar drinker who began having blackouts quite early in his alcoholic career. Most weekends and many other nights are simply beyond his ability to recall. Bill remembers often having to spend whole days trying to find where he had left his car the night before. He would have no idea of what he had said or done during those blackouts. Undoubtedly, many people had been harmed verbally and physically. Bill knows for sure there were physical hurts, because he has the morning after scars that testify to the brawls he must have been in.

Bill's house still has some holes in the plasterboard where he punched his fist in drunken rages. He once broke his wife's jaw in a blackout. She had to have the bones wired and had to eat through a straw for many weeks afterward, until she was healed. Bill can't remember a thing about it.

Then there were the many times Bill would come in, stumble around the house in the dark, and finally end up collapsing on the floor, or the bed, in his own vomit. Bill remembers none of this, except for the feelings and smells of the morning after.

When Bill sat down to speak with his wife about all this, he really didn't know where to begin. He had no idea what she would say or do. Bill said a silent prayer and began. His wife listened patiently. Bill was overwhelmed when, after he was through speaking, she hugged him and said she understood. Bill just cried. What Bill didn't realize was that his wife had also been going to a program of recovery for families of alcoholics.

The Al-Anon program is designed as a self-help support group for families of suffering alcoholics. It helps them understand the workings of alcohol and its effects upon the family. Bill's wife was also being counseled by their pastor on a regular basis, and together they had been praying for Bill's recovery. She was ready for Bill's amends and was ready to share their new life together. God's grace had sustained them both.

Scripture Study

1 John 3:18, Colossians 3:12-15

Personal Meditations:

Evening Devotion

Prayer

I thank you, O Lord, for being with me as I began to make my amends today. You took away my fears and replaced them with the love of friends. You enabled me to heal wounds of the past. I am learning so much about what it means to be reconciled. Now grant me peace this night and refreshing sleep, through Jesus Christ, my Savior. Amen

Meditation

There are a lot of things to be considered when we plan to make amends. Who all is involved in a particular hurt of the past? Though we directly hurt one person, who was hurt indirectly? As a result of something we said or did, what did that person say or do to others?

When and if we would make amends to that person, what else must be done? Would we change things for the better or for the worse? There are some things best left as they are; left for God to take care of.

Let's say, however, that the conditions are all right. We have no reason not to make the amends. What stands in the way? That old thing called fear again. This time it may include the fear of rejection. What if we try to make amends, ask for forgiveness, and then are rebuffed? Here we must make a distinction as to where the problem lies. If we have done our best with God's help to make proper amends, then the problem is borne by the other person. We can only pray that one day that person may accept our overtures and be brought to a forgiving state of spirit and mind.

There are times, however, when God provides us with special surprises. Sometimes when we approach someone to make amends, we find they have been praying for that day to come. They make us feel better about ourselves while we were planning to make them feel better. Here is where the true ministry of mutual reconciliation is indeed a joy. Here we really appreciate the gifts God gives to his people.

Finally, there are those people whom we have hurt so much that we put off approaching them, trying to figure out just how we are going to do it. This waiting can sometimes become an excuse for not doing it at all. Here again we must turn to God with repentant hearts. We must again draw that extra measure of strength from the cross and God's Spirit. We may have to go back to step three and ask ourselves just how much we have really turned our will over to the care of God. Then by God's grace we can make our amends.

Life Example

Bill had had a pretty rough time of it as alcohol really took hold of him. He lost just about everything. For years he lived in flop houses, sometimes in the street. He could hold no regular job. His employment consisted of pickup jobs as a day laborer. He'd work enough to drink, seldom anything more.

The day came when Bill did make it into a program of recovery and began working his steps. When he came to this ninth step he had quite a bit of work cut out for him. Faithfully, he began making his amends.

Included in his amends was his desire to face up to his obligations as a citizen. Bill had not filed a tax return for seven years! He had no idea what kind of penalties and fines he owed. Many weeks of those seven years were lost to him because of blackouts. But Bill gathered together what papers he could locate and headed for the office of Internal Revenue.

Bill was in for some surprises. The first one was the clerk's statement that they were only interested in his last three years of employment. The clerk took Bill's papers and made an appointment for him to return in a few days.

On the scheduled day Bill showed up, prepared for the worst. The clerk called his number and he went to the counter. The clerk looked at Bill and handed him a piece of paper. Believe it or not, according to the figures on the paper, Bill was eligible for a refund of over seven hundred dollars! He didn't have the slightest idea how this could be. He didn't argue. That money became the seed money for Bill's new life.

There is a principle that flows throughout God's Word. Whenever we think we have our life all figured out, and think it predictable, God surprises us. This is especially true when we begin to think the worst of things. Saint Paul reminds us that, when we are weak, then God's grace can really show its strength.

Scripture Study

Romans 13:7-10, Galatians 3:14-21

Personal Meditations:

Tenth Day

Morning Devotion

Prayer

O gracious God, every morning I discover new dimensions of your mercy. You have shown me your love through the love of those around me. You have shown me your forgiveness, as I have been forgiven by those I hurt in the past. Help me this day to continue in faith toward you and in love with my fellow human beings. Through Christ I pray. Amen

Meditation

We've come a long way so far. Our recovery, however, is not instantaneous. It's a process during which our old sins still cause problems, and new ones arise. We find ourselves in a lifelong process of dealing with sin and grace.

Step Ten of Alcoholics Anonymous says that we continued to take a personal inventory, and when we were wrong promptly admitted it. Back to step four? Not quite. We are not asked to rehash the old. New thoughts about the past, however, may arise and must be dealt with. Our present daily living brings with it new issues that must be faced. We find ourselves looking at our thoughts, words, and actions much more than ever before.

When under the influence, we often postponed facing our responsibilities, or avoided them altogether. Little problems that could have been solved immediately grew into big ones that became very difficult to manage. Sins left to fester can multiply into exceedingly putrid situations. The prophet compared these to flies in the ointment. Soon the whole jar of precious ointment was spoiled.

This step invites us to face up to our daily sins and deal with them immediately, before they have a chance to get out of hand. Luther saw the value in this when he wrote that, by daily contrition and repentance, the old Adam must be drowned and die and a new man daily arise and come forth.

Another factor to be considered is our past alcoholic behavior, in which we tended to pass the buck. To blame others for our own problems was not uncommon. Now, when a problem arises, we are prepared to immediately ask what our responsibility in the matter is. If something we said or did was part of the cause, then we can readily admit that and work for a solution.

As Christians, we know that we are at the same time a saint and a sinner. We no longer have to cover up our sins, but can daily face them with Christ's forgiveness and a Spirit-led resolve to remedy wrongful situations.

Life Example

Bill found it difficult enough to go back over his past sins and make his amends to those whom he had harmed along the way. It was a continual struggle to face each person he thought of as he worked his way through his program of recovery.

This step, however, was really troublesome. Bill was not used to admitting his mistakes at all, much less promptly. His was a pattern of putting things off. He kept hoping along the way that people would forget what he had done. In some cases, they did forget, but it didn't change the situation. Bill still had to live with his conscience. When he was drinking, it was somewhat numbed and forgetful. Now that Bill is sober, his past haunts his conscience. For his conscience has been fine-tuned by God's law and his moral sense of making amends has been fine-tuned by the Gospel.

Bill discussed his difficulties many times with his pastor. Slowly, he began to see how necessary it was for him to take prompt action in the present, whenever he caught himself in another sin. Otherwise, there would be another trail of one sin added to another that would build up to become a major obstacle to Bill's serenity.

Bill found the words to use. He began to say, "I'm sorry," much more often. He could say, "I think I've made a mistake." "If I've hurt you in any way, please forgive me." The more Bill practiced making his amends promptly, the more peaceful his life became. The easier it was for him to fall asleep at night. The more rested he was. The more refreshed he was each day. Serenity was a word that became meaningful to Bill.

Scripture Study

Matthew 5:23-24, Colossians 3:5-10

Personal Meditations:

Evening Devotion

Prayer

Holy Father, I pray this day that your name has been hallowed, your kingdom come, and your will done in my life as it is in heaven. I pray that I have been willing to forgive others as you have forgiven me. I am confident that I have been led from temptation and delivered from evil as you have promised to do for me. There is no other God like you. Keep me this night, I pray, according to your mercy through Jesus Christ my Lord. Amen

Meditation

How many people did we alienate simply by our refusal to promptly admit our wrongs? How different our lives would have been if fear and remorse had not stood in the way of our words and actions?

Today, God has given us new opportunities for life. As the Holy Spirit renews in us his baptismal gift of spiritual life, we find it so much easier to face people. The more we practice the principles of Christian living, the more natural such living becomes. What once felt so foreign and strange now feels more normal.

In our steps of recovery we are in the process of replacing bad habits with good ones. Theologically, we are in the process of moving from sin to righteousness, from evil to godliness. Take a look at the fifth chapter of Galatians where there is a listing of the works of the flesh and the works of the Spirit. Notice how closely the works of the flesh parallel the problems brought on by alcohol. Notice how the works of the Spirit are the desirable life we always wanted to live, and can now live by God's grace.

The continuing personal inventory is necessary so that we do not become complacent and, in so doing, make ourselves vulnerable to backsliding temptations. The stories of recovering alcoholics doing well for years and then suddenly turning back could fill volumes. Sometimes they recover once more: sometimes they don't. The danger of not returning is too great to risk not taking this important step.

To never let the sun go down on your anger is ancient, sage advice. This step also invites us to promptness in dealing with our wrongdoing. How serene our life becomes when we can go to bed at night knowing that our relationships with others are at peace. To leave personal strings dangling causes us fitful nights and increases our daytime stress. That price is too high to pay when the solution is so available. Pray God to give us the constant ability not to think of ourselves more highly than we ought to think and when wrong to promptly admit it.

Life Example

Bill had been a practicing alcoholic for some time. He always seemed to think that everyone else made mistakes, but that he was never wrong. Every job he had he lost because of his constant criticism of the people he worked for and with. However, he had always managed to get another job. The sad thing was that he was a good worker and did know his trade well. There was little in his field of work that he was incapable of doing. If he could have seen himself as others saw him, and could have admitted his shortcomings, he could have worked his way into a very successful position.

As it was, Bill decided he really had to quit working for those "other idiots" (Bill used other descriptive words). He decided to go into business for himself, be his own boss. At first this seemed like a good solution to his problems, but he couldn't run from himself.

It was not long before Bill's machinery started giving him trouble. He blamed the manufacturers. He blamed the companies that shipped the machinery, claiming damage in shipment. He blamed the people who sent him "faulty" designs. *Never* did he consider that he was at fault for anything.

One day Bill's wife called her pastor to inform him that Bill had shot and killed himself. It was a tragedy that was predictable, and yet only Bill himself held the answer to preventing it. He couldn't even live with himself. Throughout his life this Bill insisted that he could manage his life on his own. He felt he didn't really need anyone, including God. How wrong he was.

Scripture Study

Galatians 6:1-5

Personal Meditations:

Eleventh Day

Morning Devotion

Prayer

O Lord, how refreshed I am after restful sleep. How often in the past were my nights filled with fitful turnings. Your peace that passes human understanding has given me a calmness of spirit. Now may this day be one in which I may glorify your holy name through Christ, my Savior. Amen

Meditation

Step eleven of recovery states that we sought through prayer and meditation to improve our conscious contact with God, as we understood him, praying only for knowledge of his will for us and the power to carry that out. Alcoholics Anonymous is not a religious organization. Each member must seek out his answers to religious questions from his own religious affiliations.

For the Christian alcoholic, this step leads to renewed interest in God's Word and Sacraments. Contact with God is made first through God's self-revelation. The hidden God makes himself known through his Word. For our time this is the Bible.

It is still a sad fact of the modern church scene that so few members are immersed in Holy Scripture. The ancient prayer that we read, mark, learn, and inwardly digest the written Word of God evokes little response amongst the majority of church members. Small wonder then that there are so many distorted views of God's person and teachings!

To know God's will for us, to know God's complete view of life — both now and forever — is impossible without the study of God's Word. This step asks us to quit relying on half-way measures, and to sincerely search out what God has revealed to man. Here is where we also learn the heart and center of our faith, the forgiveness of sins through faith in Jesus Christ. Here we truly build on the foundation of salvation by grace, through faith in Christ, apart from works of Law.

Furthermore, for the Christian, there is provided a great source of spiritual strength in the Holy Sacraments. Baptism and the Lord's Supper are the nourishment for the soul, and are needed to sustain spiritual life as physical food is necessary for the body.

For some alcoholics, church was neglected during the drinking years. For others, church was their only tie to sanity. In either case, the church, with its means of grace and the fellowship of believers in God, becomes *The* significant nurturing source for their souls.

Alcoholics Anonymous is a program for sustaining sobriety. The Christian congregation is the source for spiritual growth. Many a person who has been willing to enter a program of recovery, but has been unwilling to return to God's Word and Sacrament, has ended in failure. They have forfeited their opportunity to obtain the power offered in the Gospel.

Life Example

Bill had had a difficult time trying to control his drinking for quite a while. He had sought help from friends, but they did not understand the disease of alcoholism. The same held true for his pastor and friends at church. Most often he was told to pray about it and just exercise more will power. Of course, that didn't work. Finally, Bill just drifted away from his church altogether, though he still maintained a personal relationship with God as best he could.

When Bill had severed his fellowship with the church, he lost a major source of possible power to resist his growing habit. Now the plunge to the bottom of his drinking increased its speed.

Eventually, Bill did hit bottom, did enter a recovery program, and started on his steps to sobriety. When he came to this step he had a problem. He remembered the attitude shown him when he sought help years before. He was not too thrilled about returning to that church. It was suggested that he nevertheless go back to his former pastor and explain what had happened.

Reluctantly, Bill visited his pastor and had a lengthy discussion with him. As a result, Bill was surprised at the pastor's willingness to ask his forgiveness for being unable to help him in the past. He was further surprised to find out that his pastor had since learned more about the problem of alcoholism, and had much more understanding of Bill's concerns. In fact, his pastor now asked if Bill could help him in dealing with some other persons who were on the verge of serious trouble with alcohol.

Bill rejoined his former congregation. He was welcomed back with joy. He renewed old friendships. Also, for the first time, he joined the adult Bible study group. He also made a resolve not to miss services of worship or neglect his attendance at the Lord's Supper. For the first time in his life Bill found the Word of God to be interesting, applicable to his real concerns, and, indeed, exciting to study.

Bill also found that the more familiar he became with the Bible, the more he realized how practical it was. The answers he had been seeking for years were suddenly popping up on the pages of Scripture as he studied. He found that when he simply sought out God's will for his life, he also found the best way to live each day.

Scripture Study

Romans 8:5-17, Philippians 3:12-15

Personal Meditations:

Evening Devotion

Prayer

Heavenly Father, how good it is to have your Word as a lamp to my feet and a light to my path. I am grateful for the assurance of your Word which does not mislead me. How easily I was misled in the past because I did not know your will for me as I should have. Thank you also for the increase of faith you give me through your Word. Amen

Meditation

We notice that the objectives of this step are two-fold. Not only do we search the Scriptures to know God's will for us, but also to find the power to carry it out. Many people remain satisfied with mere knowledge. They grow in grace and knowledge of God. They can tell you all about the fundamental teachings of the Bible. They can detail the life and work of Jesus. They can describe the mission outreach of Saint Paul. They can unravel the mysteries of the Book of Revelation. But they can't seem to translate it into action to better their own lives or the lives of others around them.

It is one thing to know God's plan of salvation through Jesus Christ. It is another to apply, through faith, that knowledge to one's soul in such a way that the feelings of guilt are washed away in the blood of the Lamb, and to see one's neighbor through the filter of the cross so we no longer judge them for their words and actions. If the Gospel is to mean anything to us at all, it must transform not only our minds, but also our hearts, souls, and lives.

Our worship is not limited to the formal services of worship in the house of God. We can worship God continually also in the arena where we live our daily life. This is why

Saint Paul could speak of praying without ceasing. Our entire day can be filled with acts of worship in which God is adored and we are absolved. There is continual confession and commitment. We are being taught and we thank him. God's sacramental blessings are showered upon us, and we respond with our sacrificial acts of thanksgiving.

This means that a continual transformation is taking place within us. More and more we are moving away from conformity with the world. God's Spirit is drawing us closer to being the imitators of Christ.

Life Example

Betty had always been active in her church. She had been involved in the youth group, the choir, and later the women's guild. Whenever there was a need for help she was there. Her attendance at worship was as regular as clockwork.

When Betty fell prey to alcohol, she couldn't believe what was happening to her. She prayed and prayed. She maintained her activity at church. Still, she kept sinking further into the habit of drinking. Try as she would, it just kept getting worse.

The guilt and remorse that Betty felt as she would sit in church was beyond description. She felt as if she were trapped in a nightmare, and wished she could wake up to find that the dream was over. She never felt deserted by God, but she did feel that she had removed herself far from his love.

When Betty finally entered into a program of recovery, she was confronted with questions of spirituality. She had always thought of herself as a spiritual person, yet now she began to reconsider what she had thought of as spiritual. The more she reflected on her past, the more she began to realize that much of her relationship to God and church were formal. She had been doing all the right things, but some-how, the deep, inner faith connection with God had not been there to the extent she now knew it must be. It wasn't as if she hadn't cared about or felt close to God. She had. But now there was something different.

Now, as she reread the Scriptures they took on new meaning for her. As she restudied the doctrines she had learned long ago, she began to see them in a new light. Her faith felt more alive to her. Her attention was now more on what she could gratefully do for God than what he could do for her in answer to her petitions. "Not my will, but thine be done." These words of Jesus now took on special mean-ing for Betty.

Scripture Study

Romans 12:1-2, 1 John 5:14

Personal Meditations:

Twelfth Day

Morning Devotion

Prayer

Again you have brought me to the beginning of another day, O Lord. How quickly these past eleven days have gone. You have been shaping and molding me for your purposes, Lord. Please continue to make me a worthy example of what your grace can do with a sinner's life. May I serve as a faithful disciple and follow you through Jesus Christ, your Son, my Lord. Amen

Meditation

The last step of the Alcoholics Anonymous program says that having had a spiritual awakening as the result of these steps, we tried to carry this message to alcoholics, and to practice these principles in all our affairs. We are reminded of Jesus' principles of discipleship. As we go along our way in life, we are to be about the business of making disciples of all people; baptizing them in the name of the Father, and of the Son, and of the Holy Spirit, and teaching them to observe all that our Lord has commanded.

These steps, used by a Christian, should lead us ever deeper into our faith in Jesus Christ and God's plan of salvation for us. Our first task in the kingdom of God is to grow into Christian maturity. Our next task is to be used by God to touch the lives of others. As alcoholic Christians we feel a particular responsibility to the active, suffering alcoholics. We can be both a power of example for them, and a source of help. Sad to say, we are still limited by their frequent refusals to listen to us — much as we used to refuse help offered to us in the past.

The term "awakening" is used in the present twelfth step. In an early draft of this step the term "experience" was used instead. We might think of it as the "enlightenment" we have as the gifts of the Holy Spirit sanctify us. The Gospel call must be enhanced by the spiritual gifts. This is Christian growth. It's the moving from milk to meat, as Saint Paul puts it. He also calls it Christian maturity.

The mature Christian simply cannot keep to himself all that he has received from God. He must share it. The disciple must become the apostle. There is an evangelistic zeal that comes from the full appreciation of God's transforming work in us. The message has to go to others.

Life Example

Bill had never been one to become too involved with others, unless it was at a party. He much preferred to let others take the lead. He was glad to help, but not direct.

When Bill began drinking excessively his withdrawal from others increased. He was either alone or lost in the crowd. People were a problem to Bill. He avoided people to avoid problems.

When Bill began his program of recovery, he slowly changed. As he worked through these steps, he found new insight into himself and his relationships with others. His experiences, as he made his amends and joined with others in his congregational activities, eventually made Bill feel more comfortable with people. People were no longer a problem to him, but opportunities for new friendships. This was all a new experience for Bill.

Bill was eager to learn how to be a helpful example to others. He learned to do this in a way that was not boastful. Through discussions with his pastor and his new friends, Bill learned ways in which he could talk to people without seeming to come on too strong. Now and then Bill's pastor began to call on him to speak to another person who was struggling with alcohol. Bill did not preach to these people, but simply shared his own experience. If they wanted help, he could suggest some steps for them to take. The decision and the action was theirs to make and to take.

Scripture Study

1 Thessalonians 5:11, 14-17

Personal Meditations:

Evening Devotion

Prayer

Dear heavenly Father, I come to you this evening with grate-fulness of heart. These twelve days have enriched my soul and lifted up my faith. You have drawn me deeper into your Word and gracious revelation of your will for me. I am learning to know you more and more as the loving and caring God that you are. Continue to lead me further into the treasures of the new life in Jesus Christ. May I be an able witness of your grace and mercy for your glory and the benefit of others. Through my Savior, Jesus, I pray. Amen

Meditation

There are recovering alcoholics who faithfully sit in meeting after meeting for years and haven't grown one bit in their sobriety. There are Christians who faithfully attend church services every Sunday and holy days for years and haven't grown one bit in their life in Christ. These are people who feel that their presence alone at these functions is sufficient. What a mistake! They are missing out on so very much. They are especially missing out on the wonderful plans God has for their lives.

This twelfth step includes two important phrases: "as a result of these steps," and "practice these principles in *all* affairs." It is great that alcoholic Christians are present at recovery meetings and worship services. However, there are programs to be worked. James said that faith without works is dead. Faith is to be functional. God's gift of grace is to have an active effect on the person. His Word is to be studied. His Sacraments are to be enriching. Unless there is posi-tive reaction to God's grace, a person ends up as a dead formalist — form, but lacking function.

In this twelfth step, we learn also that these steps of recovery extend far beyond sobriety. The alcoholic Christian especially needs to be aware that he cannot be a double-minded, double-standard person. This step demands consistency of life. These principles are to be functioning in *all* our affairs. There is no room here for "Sunday Christian" alcoholics. Jekyll and Hyde made for a fine novel, but remember that the character was self-destructive.

You might find it interesting to search through the Bible and take note of the use of words like "always," "at all times," "Everywhere," "all people," etc. There is a timelessness and all-inclusiveness about the Gospel transformation of the Christian. It's a full-time, not a part-time, life.

Life Example

Bill had been a member of Alcoholics Anonymous for many years. He attended many meetings, often going two or three times a week. He opened his door to many suffering souls. He counseled with hundreds of people. He had a reputation of having a tough-loving attitude which reached out to both the practicing and recovering alcoholic. He could be counted on to go out on twelfth-step calls at any hour of day or night.

Bill had been raised in the church, but during his drinking days had fallen away. In his years of recovery he often talked with clergy friends about religion. He indicated often to one of them that he wanted to make an appointment sometime and discuss some of his questions about church and membership. He was often reminded about his intention. The appointment was never made.

Bill's personal life was filled with troubles. Family problems, financial problems, business problems. He always said that God would see him through. Bill often spoke of

God in general. Never did Bill seem to get very specific about God. This was his real trouble. He just couldn't bring himself to settle the religious part of his life. As a result, nothing else in Bill's life seemed to get settled. He was sober, but far from serene.

Then one day, Bill's friends found that he had closed his business and left his apartment. No one could find him. It then was discovered that he had gone out drinking again. He never returned. One day Bill was found in a motel where he had hanged himself. Ironically, Bill had often told people that God had granted him his sobriety, and, if he ever went back to the bottle, he didn't think he would ever return. He was right!

Many believe the twelve steps of recovery to be God's gift to suffering alcoholics. They are meant to touch a person's life physically, mentally, emotionally, and spiritually. Bill began with the physical and the mental, and maybe a bit of the emotional. He lost sight of the spiritual and tried to go that alone. It destroyed him.

But, by God's grace, through faith in Jesus Christ, in the power of the Holy Spirit, there are tens of thousands of grateful, joyful, sober, and serene Bills and Bettys. God be praised!

Scripture Study

2 Corinthians 8:13-14, 1 John 5:1-5

Personal Meditations:

Concluding Postscript

Since you have read this far, we pray this little booklet has been of some value to your life as a sober Christian alcoholic. We are convinced that the program of Alcoholics Anonymous continues to be one of the most successful approaches to the problem of alcoholism. We are also convinced that Dr. Bob and Mr. Bill were deeply spiritual men who were at home in the Scriptures, and who intended the spiritual dimension of their program to find its fulfillment in the local parish.

The alcoholic Christian has reason to be eternally grateful for his recovery, and cannot avoid his responsibility before God as a member of Christ's church. In the fellowship of the redeemed he has a special arena for sharing his joy before the Lord.

It is also our prayer that this small book will help to fill the void of Christian devotional literature so badly needed by the recovering Christian alcoholic.

To God be the Glory

Rev. Carl Nelson
Painesville, Ohio
February 1986